The Man Who Discovered Pluto

written by Mark Dubowski
illustrated by Robert Rayevsky

It was eight o'clock and twelve-year-old Clyde Tombaugh's favorite show was beginning. It could not have been a television show, because television had not been invented.

Clyde's favorite show came on every night outside in his backyard. Clyde's favorite show was the night sky. Clyde liked to watch the moon change, to look at the stars, and to spot the planets. He could spend hours gazing at the night sky and wondering what mysteries it held.

That night, Clyde expected to see the moon, the stars, and the planets in a new way.

That night in 1918, Clyde was going to look at the sky with a real telescope. The lenses in the telescope would make distant objects look much larger.

Clyde's father had gotten the telescope for him from a mail-order catalog. It was only a little over two inches long, and it was not very powerful. But that did not bother Clyde.

He held the telescope up to his eye. When he looked through it, the craters on the moon were sharp and clear. He had never seen them like that before.

Clyde's father liked to look at the sky as much as his son. They had fun together with the telescope. But it would have been more fun if they had a better telescope, one with more powerful lenses.

Clyde's family did not have enough money to buy things like that, but Clyde and his dad had an idea.

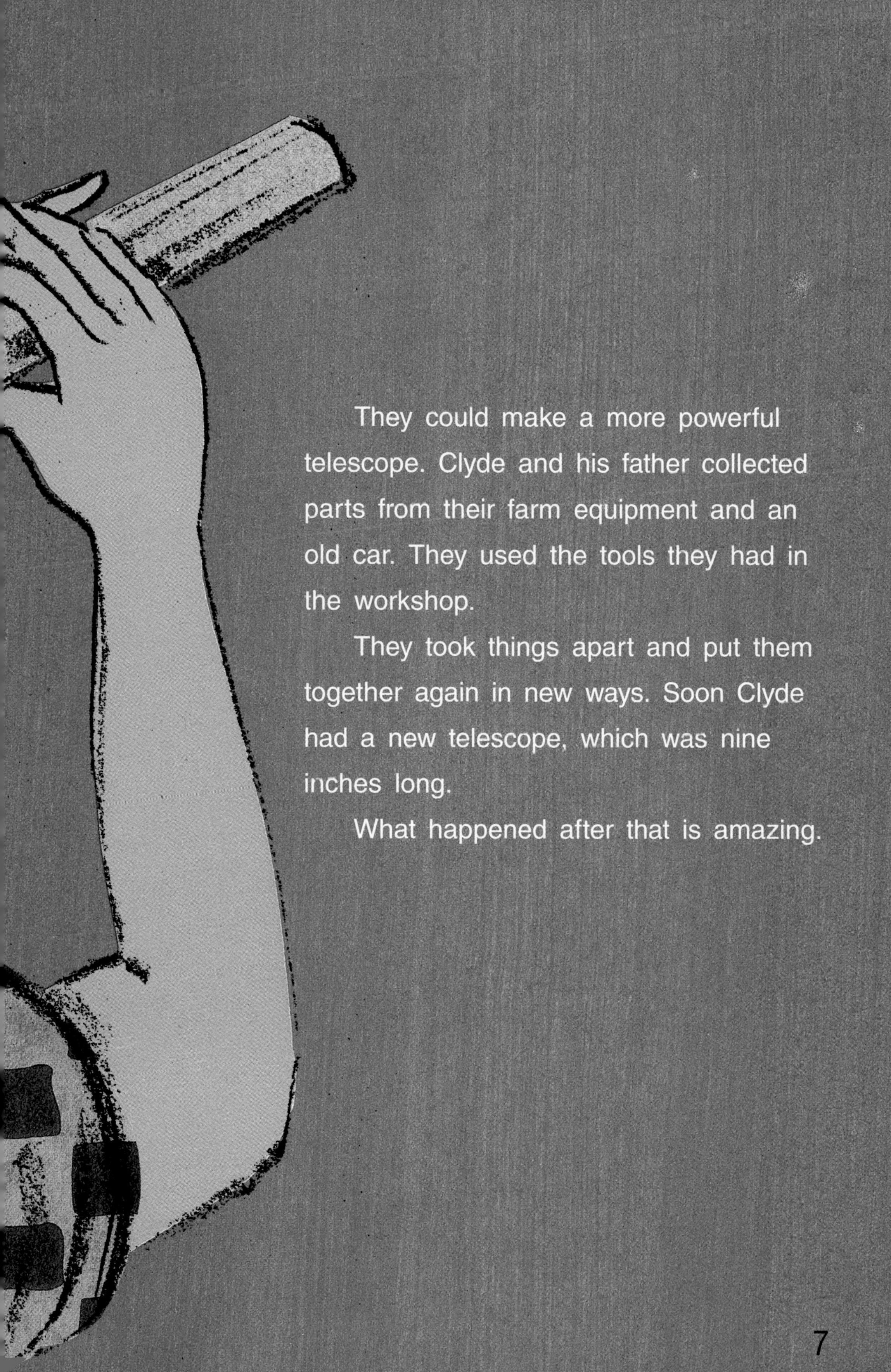

They could make a more powerful telescope. Clyde and his father collected parts from their farm equipment and an old car. They used the tools they had in the workshop.

They took things apart and put them together again in new ways. Soon Clyde had a new telescope, which was nine inches long.

What happened after that is amazing.

Right away, Clyde could see everything in the night sky much better. He aimed his homemade telescope at the moon and the stars, which looked sharp and bright. He spotted two planets and drew pictures of them. He put a label on one drawing, saying it was Jupiter. He labeled the other one Mars.

Later, he mailed the drawings and an explanation of his observations to the Lowell Observatory in Arizona. An observatory is a place with special equipment for scientists to study the universe beyond Earth. These scientists are known as astronomers.

People at the Lowell Observatory had been looking into outer space, too. They used a huge telescope that was far, far more powerful than Clyde's. But the astronomers liked Clyde's work and sent a reply to his letter. They wanted to know if Clyde would like to work at the observatory!

Of course he would! But he wasn't quite old enough to leave home. When Clyde was around 20, he went to the Lowell Observatory. They wanted him to attack the problem they called "Planet X."

Planet X was the name they had given to a planet that no one had ever seen. Astronomers believed it was on the other side of the planet Neptune, the farthest planet from Earth known to exist. Clyde's mission was to find out if Planet X was really there.

The Lowell Observatory is located high on a mountain near Flagstaff, Arizona. When the sun goes down, the temperature drops rapidly and it gets very cold. Clyde bundled up to stay warm as night after night he studied the sky. He took pictures with a camera attached to the telescope.

Day after day he pored over his pictures, searching for Planet X. Five years went by and still Clyde could not find it.

Then one day Clyde noticed in his pictures one very faint star with other stars all around it. In one picture it was in one place, and in another picture it was somewhere else.

Lowell Observatory

Observation Circular

THE DISCOVERY OF A SOLAR SYSTEM BODY APPARENTLY TRANS-NEPTUNIAN

Flagstaff, Arizona
March 13, 1930

Systematic search begun years ago supplementing Lowell's investigations for TransNeptunian planet has revealed object which since seven weeks has in rate of motion and path consistently conformed to TransNeptunian body at approximate distance be assigned. Fifteenth magnitude, Position March twelve days three hours GMT was seven seconds of time West from Delta Geminorum, agreeing with Lowell's predicted longitude.

The finding of this object was a direct result of the search program set going in 1905 by Dr. Lowell in connection with his theoretical work on the dynamical evidence of a planet beyond Neptune. The earlier searching work, laborious and uncertain because of the less efficient instrumental means, could be resumed much more effectively early last year with the very efficient new Lawrence Lowell telescope specially designed for this particular problem. Some weeks ago, on plates he made with this instrument, Mr. C. W. Tombaugh, assistant on the staff, using the Blink Comparator, found a very excepti object, which since has been stu carefully. It has been photogra regularly by Astronomer Lampland the 42-inch reflector, and also obse visually by Astronomer E. C. Sli and the writer with the large refract

The new object was first recorde the search plates of January 21 (1 23rd, and 29th, and since February has been followed closely. Besides numerous plates of it with the photographic telescope, the object been recorded on more than a sco plates with the large reflector Lampland, who is measuring both s of plates for positions of the objec rate of motion he has measured fo available material at intervals betw observations with results that appe place the object outside Neptune's at an indicated distance of about 13 astronomical units...

In brightness the object is only a 15th magnitude...neither in brigh or apparent size is the o comparable with Neptune. Prelimi

It had moved across the sky! Clyde knew it could not be a star because stars seem to move very slowly over a long period of time. It must be a planet, traveling around the sun just like Earth.

On February 25, 1930, Clyde had found Planet X. He was only twenty-four years old when he made this important discovery.

CIVIC COURTESY AND ITS CONSEQUENCES

THE simple but expressive "Please" that turned pedestrians away from a badly trampled grass border, after all other exhortations failed, has become a classic example of the efficiency of courtesy and the gently spoken word. With this in mind, perhaps, the officials of many villages located on the route of the Lincoln Highway, and elsewhere, have erected a new sort of greeting to motorists. Instead of the usual commandatory "City Limits—Slow down to 15 miles an hour," the traveler in those parts is confronted with a cordial "——— Welcomes You." And, as if to drive home the sincerity of the sentiment, the reverse side of the sign carries, for the departing visitor, a veritable pat on the back in its friendly "Good Luck. Come Again."

This is modern Applied Psychology sure enough. For few will be the motorists who will "burn up" the roads in *those* towns, or deafen their inhabitants with wide-open cut-outs or asphyxiate them with noxious gases.

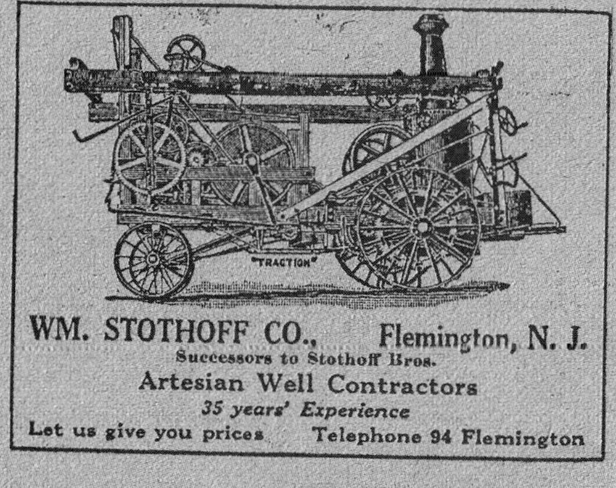

The Bay Stater

RAIN, snow, sun, and sleet! They are Time's workers of ruin to houses. If your home is built of brick, concrete, or stucco, make it waterproof and

Clyde got to name the new planet. All the other planets have names of gods from ancient Greek and Roman myths. Clyde chose the name Pluto. Pluto, the ruler of the underworld, lived hidden below the Earth. Clyde thought it was the perfect name for his planet because Pluto is hidden from sight much of the time by Neptune. That is why it took him five years to find it!

Many years later, a famous museum asked Clyde if they could have his old telescope, the one he and his father had built. They wanted it for an astronomy display. Did he still have it?

Yes, he had it in his backyard. But the museum could not have it just yet. “Sorry,” he said, “I am still using it!”